Just Some Thoughts Along the Way....
Some Might Call Them Poems

By: Kristyn T. Smith

*This collection of thoughts is dedicated to my father,
the first inspiration for my "poems",
Dennis James Smith. Thank you, Dad,
for teaching me the freedom of thought,
and encouraging my mind to explore.
Until we meet again.*

*Love,
Kris*

My First "Poem"

Thinking of You
(1993 - 11 yrs. old)

Thinking of you is what I like to do,
I remember the times we spent, our walks around the block,
but what I liked most was when you made my problems stop.

I remember when we used to talk about things we liked,
but now is not then, so we have to work on that
or else, I will eat all day and turn very fat.

But now I have to go because I want to cook
and get done reading a very good book.

Love You,
Kristyn

P.S. The fat part is supposed to be hilarious!
See ya!

Life's Journey in Ink

With pen in hand, I start the day,
writing thoughts along life's way,
each step a word, each breath a line,
in this journey, I entwine.

Pages fill with hopes and dreams,
ink flows freely, like rushing streams,
capturing moments, both bright and gray,
in the story I compose today.

Through trials faced and joys embraced,
I find my voice, my cherished space,
with every chapter, I reveal,
a tale of courage, a heart that's real.

Ink-stained fingers, weary eyes,
yet in this craft, my spirit flies,
for in the lines, I carve my path,
through love and loss, through tears and laughs.

Each scribbled note, a whispered prayer,
a testament to moments shared,
for in these words, I leave a trace,
of all I've seen, of time and place.

So let the journey twist and bend,
with pen in hand, I'll write till end,
for in this art, I find my way,
writing life, day by day.

Just a Memory

It is in my subconscious, so deep I swear it has entered my soul.
All the hopes, dreams, and prayers I had for you still unfold.

When I am in that place, my heart aches for the past.
You are so close, yet so far. It all changed so fast.

My memory had become biased and cloudy,
but oh, that subconscious—it can only tell the truth,
as in my dreams it is the real you.

That feeling of smallness, worthlessness and fear
that I know all too well has returned.
So strong that reality is hard to discern.

This is not yearning in my heart,
this is burning in my heart.

It cannot be that I miss how you made me feel.
That would be insane,
a true malfunctioning of my mind, of my brain.

When I watch "our" story though my subconscious eye,
self-doubt and self-loathing is all I can see,
as there was no love, no respect, no trust, nor any passion for me.

I guess I thought it might just be,
if only I could work my magic for the world to see.

When all is said and done, what will be, will be.
But you know what?
That magic did happen—only it happened with ME.

I don't actually miss you;
I miss the "what could be".
But it is all over now, because you are just a memory .

Eyes Of A Loner

Don't look at me, for my eyes can not lie.
I mustn't be exposed.
Please just pass me by.
Today I have eyes of a loner,
and they are likely to cry.

The quiet has become much too loud.
Living in my mind is like living on a cloud.

Floating above the world,
where all is observed.
Never taking part.
To most this is absurd.

But you see, detachment has its comforts.
Dwelling here, I am safe.
I can no longer create new memories,
that can never be erased.

Such a perfect little remedy
that will always protect,
as there is too much at risk
for me to again connect.

Longing for Authenticity

I struggle in a world where one's emotions are fair game.
Where relationships are shallow and taken in vain.

I struggle in a world where vulnerability is weakness,
Where no one is willing to put down their defenses.

I long for a world where kindness is the norm, not the exception.
Where being flawed is seen as perfection.

I long for the day when someone will know the real me.
Not my many outer levels, but what lies beneath.

I long for the day that I am spotted in the crowd.
My true colors blazing so incredibly loud.

It's Just You

In a crowd full of beauty, wealth, power, and fame,
what you focus on puts them to shame.
It's just you.

When life throws its sharpest daggers,
they never pierce my soul,
as I am shielded by the love that flows from you that makes me whole.

The power you possess in my life is purely enchanting.
Never ceasing to amaze me.
Your power allows me to see myself through your eyes.
So beautiful, so sexy, the absolute prize.

I am ready to take on the world.
Not that validation is needed,
but what a high when I see the way you gaze at me.
A gaze of love that sets my spirit free.

That smirk you give carries a deeper meaning.
You know how lucky you are.
For all you feed my soul,
I nourish you just the same.
You are the SOUL source provider of my heart's flame.
It's just you.

I am far from perfect, but in your eyes, perfection in the making.
We are perfect complements for what each of us is lacking.
It's a continuous dialogue of learning between you and me.
We challenge one another continuously.
Together, we are both the winner.

No words are needed to define what I mean to you.
Your touch tells it all, your eyes tell the world.
The lines crossed by imposters in the past
don't even exist to you.
And each day I am amazed by the wonder of you.

You never want to hurt me, for I give you strength.
I feel safe in your arms,
as your embrace carries me through the days with confidence.
It's just you.

The Inconsistent One

There can be but only one way the soul for me is to love…..
that is with consistency.
Else, it can't possibly define the absoluteness of love, of the divine.
Fair weather-ness has no place in this space.
Oh, inconsistent one, I can see your intentions written all over your face.
What lies beneath is far more complex than what meets the eye.
An endless smile with an affinity to please,
gave you the idea that it doesn't take much to capture my heart,
and that mere words are all you would need.
I must admit, sweet words can be music to lonely ears.
But if you listen long enough, you'll hear that melody fade, then disappear.

Again We Meet

Again we meet.

I stand out like a star against the midnight sky.

That look in their eyes ignites such a sensation within me.

Only THAT look.

I am not anxious. I am not self-conscious. I am not alone.

They are seeing the "me" inside that no one else has managed to see.

I've never felt so feminine, so sexy, so beautiful.

My skin feels like mine. I own it.

Who are these mysterious figures stirring this cosmic storm in my soul?

I can nearly see them....one final squint....It's Confidence.

"Hello, nice to see you again".

And standing right behind her, I see Love.

"My, have I been missing you two in my life as of late!"

Who knew that running into these two would be so revolutionary

to my soul, to my being, to my eyes?

We embrace tightly, and as we part, they gently whisper,

"We 'see' you, Kristyn. Now, with our help, it's time for you to 'see' yourself".

Sanctuary of Solitude

In the quiet corners of my mind,
where solitude and stillness intertwine,
I find solace in the depths unseen,
a world where silence reigns serene.

Amidst the bustling crowds, I stand,
an introvert in a vast expanse,
observing, listening, absorbing the scene,
yet often longing for a quiet stream.

In the company of my thoughts, I dwell,
where words unspoken gracefully swell,
each moment a treasure, a whispered retreat,
where introspection and reflection meet.

My heart, a sanctuary, a sacred space,
where solitude's embrace finds its place,
for in the quiet of solitude's embrace,
I find my strength, my inner grace.

Though misunderstood, I stand secure,
in the beauty of my nature, pure,
for in the silence, I find my voice,
a quiet strength, a gentle choice.

So let the world buzz and chatter on,
in solitude's embrace, I am drawn,
for in the depths of introverted grace,
I find my home, my sacred space.

A Father's Whispers

In the whispers of a memory so dear,
a little girl with skates, filled with fear.
Her father's voice firm and clear,
threatened to take them if she didn't dare.

With a deep breath, she took the chance,
gliding down the hill in a rhythm dance.
His words ringing in her ears,
propelling her forward, erasing her fears.

Life's challenges like hills to climb,
her father's warning a reminder in time.
To face the unknown, to push through,
his love and guidance forever true.

Dear father, your lessons still ring,
in every challenge, your voice does sing.
Threats turned to motivation so grand,
guiding me gently with a firm hand.

Though you're gone, your spirit remains,
in every triumph, in life's terrain.
With skates on my feet, and courage in my heart,
I'll conquer the hills, never to part.

As time unfolds its mysterious tale,
I'll carry your wisdom, I'll set sail.
Through valleys and peaks, through stormy weather,
your words of strength bind us together.

In the echoes of laughter, in the tears that fall,
your presence lingers, embracing all.
So here's to you, my guiding light,
in every challenge, in every fight.

With skates on my feet,
I'll glide with grace,
remembering your words in every race.
For in each obstacle, each daunting hill,
your love and wisdom guide me still.

I love you, Dad

Make Me Something New

In the quiet of the morning's hue,
I whisper softly, "Make me something new."

Shed the layers of my worn-out skin,
let the transformation gently begin.

Take the fragments of my yesterdays,
weave them into brighter ways,

Stitch my heart with threads of light,
guide me through the darkest night.

With every breath, I yearn to grow,
to let the winds of change bestow.

A sense of purpose, clear and true,
to craft a self that's fresh and new.

Shape my thoughts like sculpted clay,
mold my fears and doubts away,

Paint my dreams in vibrant hues,
inspire paths I dare to choose.

Make me resilient, strong, and kind,
leave the past, no longer blind,

With courage as my guiding star,
transform me into who you are.

Renew my spirit, heal my scars,
lead me toward the distant stars.

In the quiet of the morning's hue,
I whisper softly, "Make me something new."

Strength in Solitude

In the quiet hours before dawn's first light,
she rises, weary, yet ready to fight.
With strength and grace, she faces each day,
a single mother, finding her way.

The nights are long, the days a blur,
every moment dedicated to her,
She feels the weight of every chore,
yet in her heart, she's something more.

The pain of loneliness often stings,
missing the comfort a partner brings.
But in her children's eyes, so bright,
she finds her purpose, her guiding light.

The endless tasks, the constant grind,
leave little time for peace of mind.
Yet in the chaos, love is sown,
in every moment, her strength is shown.

She carries dreams both big and small,
for herself and her children, she'll give her all.
Through every struggle, through every tear,
her love remains, true and clear.

The joy of first steps, the sound of their laughter,
moments of bliss she's forever after.
In every hug, in every kiss,
she finds a world of boundless bliss.

*The weight of worry often bears down,
concerns of the future, of smiles turned to frowns.
Yet she marches on, with a heart so true,
every challenge faced, she finds something new.*

*Her children see her as their hero,
her love, a force, that makes them grow.
In scraped knees and childhood stories,
she finds the heart of life's glories.*

*In quiet moments when they're asleep,
she allows herself a chance to weep.
Tears of exhaustion, of fears unspoken,
but also of love, a bond unbroken.*

*Her sacrifices, silent and deep,
promises made, she always keeps.
The world may see her as just one,
but to her children, she's the sun.*

*They draw from her, strength and grace,
a loving heart, a warm embrace.
Her courage, a beacon in the night,
guiding them with gentle light.*

*She dreams of days, both near and far,
when her efforts shine just like a star.
Her children grown, strong and kind,
proof of the strength she left behind.*

Though she walks this path alone,
her love has built a sturdy home.
With every step, her spirit grows,
a testament to the life she chose.

In the end, she finds her peace,
in the love that will never cease.
A single mother, brave and true,
her story one of strength renewed.

The Dance of a Lifetime

Life, a timeless dance,
unfolding in rhythms known and unknown,
from the innocent steps of childhood's wonder,
to the soul-searching strides of youth's exploration.

Adulthood summons with its harmonies,
a blend of responsibilities and aspirations,
navigating the currents of love and loss,
weaving resilience into the fabric of our being.

Days flow like melodies,
each moment a note in our evolving composition,
in the dance of life, we find meaning,
in the echoes of laughter and tears.

The cadence of existence, ever-changing,
a reflection of our journeys and discoveries,
through trials and triumphs,
we uncover the depths of our souls.

And as the dance gently slows,
we embrace the memories etched in our hearts,
for in the dance of life, we come to see,
the beauty of life's sweet symphony.

The Weight of Approval

In the mirror's reflection, I see,
a face shaped by worry, not truly me.
Anxiety whispers its endless demands,
tying my heart with invisible strands.

I wear a mask, a smile in place,
hiding the turmoil, the inner chase.
Every word, every glance, a plea,
for acceptance, for someone to see.

I dance to the tune of others' needs,
ignoring my own heart as it pleads.
Bending, twisting, to fit their mold,
trading authenticity for approval's cold hold.

My thoughts race, my heart pounds,
in the silence, my doubt resounds.
"What if I fail? What if I fall?"
The fear of rejection, the heaviest thrall.

I seek validation in every smile,
in every nod, I travel miles.
Yet the more I strive, the more I lose,
myself in the crowd, in their varied views.

People-pleasing, a double-edged sword,
cuts through my spirit, leaves me ignored.
For in trying to be what others demand,
I lose the courage to take a stand.

Anxiety grips me, tight and fierce,
its claws dig deep, my soul is pierced.
But in the quiet, a voice remains,
a whisper of truth through all the strains.

To break these chains, to find my way,
I must learn to live for myself each day.
To speak my truth, to show my face,
to find within the strength and grace.

Approval may come, approval may go,
but my worth is something only I can know.
In the heart of the storm, I'll find my peace,
reclaim my life, and let the need to please cease.

My Plus Ten

Ten years ahead, you paved the way,
a sister, a friend, forever to stay.
You were there to raise me, teach me, and help me grow,
through every high and every low.

Not just blood, but a bond so true,
we grew together, me and you.
Through teenage trials, joy, and pain,
you were my shelter in the rain.

Ten years apart, but closer in heart,
from the very beginning, you played a special part.
Not just a sister, but a hand to hold,
a heart so warm, yet fierce and bold.

You helped me flourish and shape who I've become,
not just as family, but my biggest fan from day one.
Together we laughed, together we cried,
side by side, always, with nothing to hide.

So here's to you, my sister, my guide,
with you, my soul will always reside.
In this life and beyond, I'd choose you again,
my sister, my forever friend, my plus ten.

Awakening

In this life, I awaken, shaking off the heavy cloak of fear and doubt, and stepping into the light of spiritual discovery. The old layers peel away, revealing the essence of my true self, tender and resilient. Spiritual whispers guide me through the shadows, illuminating paths once hidden in the darkness of my mind. Each breath, each heartbeat, becomes a sacred rhythm, a step toward the boundless sea of enlightenment.

I find myself in harmony with the universe, feeling its pulse within my soul, and recognizing the celestial thread woven through every moment. Nature's symphony sings to me, the rustling leaves, the showering rain, all echoing the truths I am just beginning to understand. In the silence of meditation, in the stillness of dawn, I connect deeply with the essence of existence, finding peace and clarity.

This journey is not without its trials, but with every stumble, I learn, grow, and rise. I embrace the lessons, the joys, and the pains, each one a brushstroke on the canvas of my awakening. This life, this precious journey, becomes a dance of the soul, a harmonious blend of seeking and finding, of questions and answers, leading me ever closer to the divine within and around me.

The Uninvited Guest

I never invited you in,
yet you've been here for years.
Such a selfish co-habitant,
feeding off my fears.

You make your presence known at the absolute worst of times.
I try to ignore you,
but you take control of my body and mind.

You are there for all moods...happy, sad, and in between,
causing my body to react as if it's fleeing a scene.
Heart racing, clothes are drenched,
I swore this was to happen only when things got intense.

Not when I am sharing a happy memory,
or just speaking from the heart.
You twist my words, you cloud my thoughts,
tearing my peace completely apart.

In the silence of the night,
when all should be at rest,
you whisper doubts and fears,
turning calm into distress.

I long for the day when you aren't here,
when my mind is my own, free and clear.
But you are relentless, never letting go,
a shadow in the light, a storm uncontrolled.

I fight daily to free myself,
and silence your cruel voice,
to use the strength within my soul,
and make a different choice.

For though you linger,
though you stay,
I know it will not forever be this way.

I'll find my peace,
I'll find my calm,
And finally feel that I belong.

In Her Footsteps

I watched you navigate each day,
independence lighting your way.
In the quiet strength you showed,
a path to grace in me was sowed.

You moved through life with steady hand,
teaching me to understand
that true strength is often found
in silent steps on solid ground.

I saw you face the world alone,
with courage in each undertone.
No need for words, your actions spoke,
in every challenge you awoke.

Your grace in handling life's demands,
in every task, your calm commands,
Showed me how to be composed,
when facing life's unending throes.

You taught me how to stand up tall,
to trust myself through rise and fall.
Your independence was my guide,
a beacon that I hold inside.

I learned that strength is standing firm,
unshaken through each twisting turn.
By watching you, I came to see
the power of humility.

Now, as I walk my chosen way,
I carry with me every day
the lessons that you've lived and shown,
in your shadow, I have grown.

Thank you, Mom, for all you've done,
for showing me the strength of one.
Through you, I've learned to face my fears,
with grace and strength throughout the years.

I love you, Mom.

My Tribe

In life's journey, so wide and vast,
a few souls I met became connections fast.
With a glance and a few words, I knew them well,
in their presence, my heart could tell.

They understand me without a word,
in their silence, my voice is heard.
Through laughter, tears, and quiet nights,
long conversations with deep insight.

Connections of this magnitude
are few and far between.
For an introvert like me,
an absolute dream.

They stand by me, through thick and thin,
my chosen family, not just friends.
In their presence, I find my peace,
my worries fade, my anxieties cease.

Here's to the bonds that time can't break,
to the memories, old and new, that we'll make.
In my tribe, I've found my place,
and in their hearts, my safe space.

K3

In the sky of my heart, three stars gleam bright,
each one unique, each a source of light.

The first, a beacon of art, introverted and deep,
her soul whispers secrets she quietly keeps.
In her world of colors, her visions take flight,
a collage of dreams painted in the night.
She too, finds peace in words and song,
and in her own rhythm, she is strong.

The second, a butterfly, beautiful and grand,
a natural leader with a guiding hand.
Her presence commands and her beauty shines,
social yet kind, she truly defines.
She lights up the world with a simple smile,
lifting our spirits in her playful style.

The third, inquisitive, with a voice that rings clear,
loves to sing, her melodies sincere.
In the heart of the family, she finds her peace,
her joy in togetherness never does cease.
Curious and vibrant, her questions unbound,
in her eagerness for knowledge, her answers are found.

Three celestial bodies, each a part of me,
my amazing daughters, my cherished K3.

To My Inner Child

Hey there, little one, come close and hear,
I know you've been carrying so much fear.
With your big bright eyes and heart so pure,
we're on a journey to find our cure.

I see the hurt, the tears you've shed,
the heavy thoughts inside your head.
But now it's time to let it go,
to heal those wounds, to let love flow.

Hold my hand, we'll take it slow,
step by step, together we'll grow.
I'll be the friend that you need,
with every hug, I'll sew a loving seed.

Remember how you loved to play?
How the world felt on a summer day?
We'll bring that joy back to your life,
until your heart feels full and bright .

When you feel scared, just call my name,
I'm here to soothe, to ease the pain.
We'll chase away the shadows deep,
and find the dreams you thought to keep.

So dry your tears and lift your chin,
together, child, we will win.
With love and care, we'll heal the past,
and build a bond that's made to last.

My inner child, so brave and true,
I'm here to heal and comfort you.
In every smile and tender touch,
we'll find the peace we've wanted so much.

Capricorn & Scorpio

We crossed paths in the high school haze,
two different signs, set in our ways.
Capricorn grounded, with plans and goals,
Scorpio mysterious, with secrets untold.

I am the planner, careful and slow,
you live more in the moment, letting it flow.
Where I see walls, you see the skies,
where I am cautious, you challenge to rise.

Your passion pushes me to take the leap,
to dive into dreams, no matter how deep.
You teach me to trust in the unknown,
that not every step needs to be shown.

You balance my earth with your waves of might,
a beautiful contrast, like day to night.
Capricorn steady, Scorpio wild,
in this friendship, we're perfectly styled.

Years have passed, but nothing's changed,
our bond is strong, our sisterhood remains.
So many obstacles, yet we still stand,
Capricorn and Scorpio, hand in hand.

We're not just friends; we're a cosmic blend—
Capricorn and Scorpio, until the end.

The Flirty Life

There comes a time in life when lessons are embraced.
In this kingdom, peace of mind, happiness, and joy reign supreme.
Self-assurance and confidence, the rewards of storms weathered
and challenges overcome.
These unspoken truths guide us toward abundance,
sparking self-reflection and lighting the path to wisdom.
For some, the chapter of hard knocks may play on a loop,
perhaps because they've only skimmed the highlights,
missing the depth found in the original text.
By the midpoint of one's story,
another may just be starting chapter one.
But the ultimate goal is universal: to get it right.
To live the flirty life.

Free

I am free to dream beyond the skies,
to chase the stars, to rise, to fly.

I am free to love with an open heart,
unburdened by the past, a fresh new start.

I am free to help, to lift, to care,
to show the world that I am there.

I am free to laugh, to cry, to be,
to speak my truth in its entirety.

I am free to think and trust my mind,
to leave all doubts and fears behind.

I am free to see the world my way,
to wander and find wonder, every waking day.

I am free to heal, to grow, to learn,
to watch the tides of life return.

I am free to follow my own pace,
to carve my path, to find my grace.

I am free to rest, to pause, to breathe,
to dance, to dream, to just believe.

I am free to sing my song aloud,
to stand up tall, to stand so proud.

I am free to cherish all that's near,
to forgive, and let go of fear.

I am free to ask, to seek, to find,
to shape my life, to free my mind.

I am free to live in boundless light,
to awaken my soul, and soar to new heights.

I am free to be exactly me,
unashamed, unchained, and standing boldly.

Closing Thoughts:

I want to express my deepest gratitude to you, dear reader, for taking the time to explore this collection of personal thoughts. Our thoughts and our take on the world are what make us beautifully unique. They are also what makes us free. I hope that these thoughts have resonated with you in some way.

It has been a journey of introspection, emotion, and sharing, and I am thankful for your companionship through these pages.

May the sentiments expressed in these "poems" stay with you, offering moments of reflection, comfort, and connection.

Thank you for being a part of my journey.

~Kristyn T. Smith

I am a mother, daughter, sister, and friend on a transformative journey of wellness and peace. As a passionate advocate for positive thinking, I am on a quest to empower others, as well as myself, to reach new heights by cultivating a positive mindset. Through prompted positive affirmation journals, poems, short stories, and self-reflection books, I aspire to inspire and guide individuals on their path to greater well-being, peace, and joy.

Love this book?

Check out more titles by
scanning this QR code!